THE SAMPLER QUILT WORKBOOK

THE SAMPLER QUILT
WORKBOOK

Dinah Travis

St. Martin's Press
New York

THE SAMPLER QUILT WORKBOOK. Copyright © 1990 by Dinah Travis

ISBN 0 312–04133–0

First published in Great Britain by B.T. Batsford Limited

First U.S. Edition
10 9 8 7 6 5 4 3 2 1

Typeset by Deltatype, Ellesmere Port, S. Wirral
and printed in Hong Kong

Contents

Acknowledgement

I would like to express my thanks to Pat Salt for her support over the planning of the original course on which this book is based and for reading the text for technical detail. Thanks also to my husband for painstakingly reading the original text, and to Adele Corcoran for reading the text for the use of English-American vocabulary. My appreciation goes to Moyra McNeill, who encouraged me to write the book and for introducing me to B. T. Batsford, whose staff have been understanding with a first-time author; to Margot Stonestreet for allowing me to reproduce her quilt on the title page, and to the students of the Bromley Adult Education Service for their ideas and enthusiasm, and for the loan of their quilts.

Introduction

What is a quilt? A quilt is layers of cloth stitched together enclosing padding between the layers.

What is a sampler quilt? A sampler quilt is a quilt which has a number of different ideas in it. These could be a lot of different patterns, a collection of different fabrics or an illustration of several different techniques used by the patchworker or quiltmaker. The quilt made in this book is a sampler quilt made up of many patterns, which will be referred to as blocks throughout the book. Needlewomen have made samplers using their own speciality for generations. It is a way of learning and of recording knowledge already learned.

The method of constructing a quilt described in this book is known as 'quilt-as-you-go', or lap quilting. Small areas of a quilt are assembled and quilted in the hand, as against a whole quilt being mounted on a large quilting frame. It is a method suited to the modern way of life because the work remains in small units that are easily quilted to this stage in the hand and are only joined into one large quilt at the last stage. The quiltmaker can easily carry a small unit around and work on it in an odd moment. Details will be found in the chapter on techniques.

This book does not tell you with precise measurements how to put a quilt together, but encourages even the most inexperienced to design your own quilt by taking you through the necessary thinking process to produce a pleasing and personal quilt of the size and colour that you like, and one that is not quite like any other, although you may be using many of the same basic ideas.

This thinking can be applied to designing any other quilt if you find yourself caught up in the mystique of quiltmaking. I hope that I will have encouraged you to extend your knowledge about fabric, pattern, and colour as you make decisions about the design and the construction of your quilt, that you will be more versatile in your thoughts about quiltmaking and that you will have confidence to approach the making of any quilt no matter what colour or size, or for whom you are making it.

The designs used in this book are based on or derived from blocks found in traditional quilts from Britain and America, along with variations and patterns that you could have designed yourself. The designs have been well tried and tested by many students and will be suitable whether the quilt is for a bed or a wall hanging, large or small. There is a wealth of ideas in the old quilts, and in using the idea of a sampler quilt we are continuing the craft of quiltmaking and creating a new generation of heirlooms.

4 Sampler quilt containing all the twenty-five blocks constructed in the book using a wide range of pink cotton fabrics. The blocks are 12in square and note that all the individual quilt borders are of a different print. Quilt made by the author

1

Requirements for making a quilt

The main requisite for making a quilt is a love of fabrics and pattern. It is helpful to have the urge to create something with the fabrics, whether it be an extra large quilt for a kingsize bed or a miniature quilt for a doll's house. Sometimes it is necessary to begin sewing even though the finished quilt is not always clear in your mind.

It is possible to make a quilt from a rag-bag of scraps and using the simple, everyday sewing tools available in the home, as must have been done in the poor homes of Ireland or the North-East of Britain in the nineteenth century. So it is not essential to spend a large sum of money on the latest fashion in fabrics or on gadgets such as a new quilting frame. Do, however, go out and buy fabrics in the sales, at the large city stores, in the market or in the local shop if that is what you require, and even invest in a quilting frame if that is what suits you.

The quilt in this book is made with the simplest of equipment and materials, and following is a general list of the requirements:

The usual sewing tools: needles, sewing thread, pins, thimble, tape measure, scissors and a soft pencil
A table to work at and lay out your work on
A board on which to pin out your blocks while in progress
An iron and ironing board
A sewing machine for those who have the urge to progress quickly
A supply of card which is easily cut with scissors
Drawing tools: a hard pencil, a ruler, a rubber, a pair of compasses, a protractor, scissors for cutting card
A supply of cotton fabrics
An interlining
A large flat area where you can lay out the complete quilt

Each individual with sewing experience will know instinctively what will be required and will be able to adjust to any new need while learning the techniques of quiltmaking.

2

Planning the quilt

Measurements

The size of a quilt can be a very daunting prospect, and this problem will only be resolved by making good plans. It is necessary to make a few decisions about the quilt. Where will it be housed? Is it to be for a single or a double bed? Is the quilt intended for an unusual place such as a wall or to cover a piece of furniture? Will the quilt be rectangular or square? I find square quilts are very versatile because they are more adaptable and fit a place in any direction. For example, a quilt that is exposed to sunlight will fade: it is useful to be able to turn it around and therefore subject it to a consistent amount of fading. It is very difficult to eliminate all the conditions that contribute to the loss of colour by fading, but at least the quilt can be designed to minimize this.

You can now decide on the overall size of the quilt. Having made that decision, consider how many blocks you require and of what size. Give each block a border for ease of construction in the 'quilt-as-you-go' method. This border is sometimes called a lattice. Make up your mind at this stage on whether the entire quilt needs a border. Now you are ready to draw yourself a plan of your quilt on paper, for reference while constructing. It is easier to use graph or squared paper to do this. Decide on a scale – for example, does the small square equal an inch or a centimetre? – then draw your plan.

There are two plans illustrated here. The pink quilt plan has twenty-five 12in × 12in (30cm × 30cm) blocks, each with a 2in (5cm) border and a 3in (7cm) border round the quilt, the overall measurement being 86in (215cm) square. The blue quilt plan has twelve 6in × 6in (15cm × 15cm) blocks each with a 1½in (4cm) border and a 6in (15cm) border round the quilt, the overall measurement being a 39in × 48in (100cm × 120cm) rectangle.

It is advisable to keep a record of all the decisions taken while constructing the quilt because even a short break in a working period can put an idea out of the mind. I make a note of such details as the length of the stitch used on my machine and the width of any seam allowances to be made, together with costs, yardages and the time I expect to spend on each stage.

Colour

The choice of colour is very personal. The colour for your quilt will depend on for whom you are making it or in which environment it is to be placed. A quilt intended for the bed of an elderly aunt will perhaps be of a quieter nature than one destined for a wall of a public building or a child's nursery. A quilt with dark and light toned colours will give a lively feel, as will the use of primary colours (reds, blues and yellows) or the use of contrasting colours (red and

5 A quilt plan with twelve 6in by 6in blocks each with a 1½in border and a 6in border around the quilt, the overall measurement being a 39in by 48in rectangle

6 A quilt plan with twenty-five 12in by 12in blocks each with a 2in border and a 3in border around the quilt, the overall measurement being 86in square

green or yellow and purple). If you want a quilt that pleases quietly and gently, then choose colours in a limited tonal range, either all dark or all pale, to take up the colours in the quilt's eventual home. It is good to have some contrast in the colour scheme, even if only very small, especially if the quilt is to be in a position in which it is intended to be a main feature of a room and therefore eye-catching.

One way of securing a pleasing result when you have no particular scheme to follow is to take two colours and to select other colours very close to these. If you choose red and green, then add red-purples, red-oranges, green-yellows and green-blues, but eliminate true blues and true yellows. Alternatively, the two colours originally chosen can be close in relation to each other, and then the whole colour scheme will appear united and soft.

The borders around the individual blocks and that around the whole quilt need to be considered when thinking about the colour scheme. The borders around the individual blocks give the opportunity to unite the colour within any one block as the quilt progresses. The border around the whole quilt can then bring an overall unity.

Fabrics

There are other considerations besides colour to be made when selecting fabrics: for example, should one use a mixture of types of fabric? It is inadvisable to use fabrics of different composition together. For example, cotton fabrics do not react sympathetically with poly-cotton fabrics.

11

In some cases there may be reasons for using various fibres together, but be sure you know exactly what that reason is and what pitfalls there may be, if any.

There is no reason why you should not use small prints alongside large prints, or regular prints, such as dots or stripes, alongside free-flowing prints, such as rambling flowers. Use prints and plain fabrics to create the mood you require as you would do with colours. Contrasting prints will give you a lively feel. Regular prints together will give an orderly, precise and safe feeling. Florid prints together give a feeling of movement.

I try to use a variety of fabrics in both colour and print to produce a harmony of colour, tone and design. The more fabrics that are introduced round a colour scheme or shape, the greater the feeling of unity. It is very difficult to buy all the fabrics in one go, so the more fabrics you are prepared to use, the easier it is to introduce the odd one while the quilt is in progress. I take about eighteen months to assemble the range of fabrics for a quilt. Of course it is possible to go out and buy a limited and co-ordinating range of fabrics in one shopping expedition at shops that cater especially for the more timid of us, but this will make a less individual quilt.

Quality of fabric

The quality of fabric you use will depend on those you like, or those that match the scheme, or those that are readily available. If you are using a substantial interlining such as the Terylene wadding, this makes the process of mixing different weights of fabrics easier because the wadding helps to even out the weight. But be careful, because it is difficult to sew a fine cotton lawn to a furnishing cotton, even for those experienced in handling fabrics, and seams can easily drag.

Interlinings

Man-made Terylene wadding interlining is the most convenient to use because it is the one most readily available in local fabric shops. It comes in a variety of thicknesses. The thinnest is 2oz (50gm); 4oz (100gm) is twice as thick; 6oz (150gm) is three times as thick, and so on. There are many different types of interlining that may be used. An old blanket, a flannelette sheet, domette, carded wool, silk or cotton wadding are all interlinings that have been used for quilts. Make sure you know how to deal with the type of interlining you choose, and consult the manufacturer if you have any doubts. Cotton wadding and carded wool are two that have been widely used in England in the past, but their

chief disadvantage is that you must do considerably more quilting to keep the wadding stable, especially if you intend that the quilt should be well used and laundered.

Fabric quantity

A rough estimate of how much fabric you need for your quilt can be made by calculating the area of the quilt, by multiplying the width of the quilt by the length. If the quilt is 3 yards by 3 yards (3m $\times$ 3m), then the area is 9 square yards (9m^2). Add to this a third as much again, which makes 12 square yards (12m^2): this is approximately the amount of fabric you will need for the top surface of the quilt, for example about 12 yards (12m) of 36in (90cm) wide fabric or 9½ yards (9½m) of 45in (112cm) wide fabric. This is only a very rough way of estimating. The more seams you have, the more fabric you will require. Consider whether you need to make an estimate for the fabrics required for the borders of the blocks and the border of the whole quilt. You will also have to make an estimate for the backing fabric and the interlining. Remember there will be seams to be put into these calculations too. I always over-estimate on my fabric calculations because I know that any fabric left over will be sewn into another quilt in the future. If you choose to be economical in purchasing your fabrics, be prepared to introduce different fabrics into the quilt as the work progresses.

Threads

Use a sewing thread that suits you and your sewing machine. I would recommend you use the one you are used to. Choose a quilting thread after trying out a few. My experience is that one person will like the feel of one thread and another will not. I prefer my thread not to be too springy, and therefore use a 100 per cent cotton thread. There are a variety of different cotton threads that can be used, such as crochet cotton or 50 sewing thread. The thickness will depend on the fabrics through which I am quilting.

Needles

Experiment by quilting with various sizes and lengths of needles on a sample of the thickness of the quilt, and use whichever needle feels comfortable for you. Most beginners prefer a firm long-eyed, long needle, but those with experience use a short, small-eyed and sharp-pointed needle.

7 *The colour quilt with a colour plate top left, contrasting colour schemes, harmonious colour schemes, tonal colour schemes, a pale scheme and a dark scheme*

Progress

The individual blocks can be made as single units for colour and design, but it will be necessary to make an assessment of the progress of the quilt by laying out the completed blocks to compare their use of colour and fabrics and to see whether any adjustment to the balance is needed in the overall plan. Compare the blocks after completing perhaps four or five, and then again after eight or ten, and so on until all the blocks are completed. It might be found that an extra colour is needed, or that a dark-toned fabric would help to create the required effect. Do not be surprised if you find that you change your mind about the use of colour and tone. Most quiltmakers start out being very careful in their selection of fabrics and then, as they gain momentum in the work and get more excited, the colours become brighter and more contrasting in tone. Do not abandon the first tentative blocks at this stage. Every block will have a place in the final arrangement of the quilt.

Do not forget to make a note of all your decisions as you go along.

13

3

Techniques

Drawing the block

The blocks must be drawn up accurately and to the correct size for your quilt. Have the basic tools ready before you embark on the drawing:

A hard, sharp pencil (H)
A ruler long enough to draw the diagonal of the block
A pair of compasses
A protractor
A good plastic rubber
Card that is firm, but easily cut with scissors

Most blocks fit into a grid or some basic structure, and this can be enlarged or reduced to suit the requirements of your quilt. There are a number of different blocks illustrated in the main section of this book. Guidance on how to draw them in detail is accompanied by variations and other blocks that are similar in construction.

First draw the square of your block to the correct size, being sure to draw it with accurate right-angled corners on card. Find the correct grid or structure for the block and draw this within the square. Draw the lines of the block into the grid or structure following the illustration or instruction. Make a drawing to keep for reference while constructing the block.

In some of the drawings it is necessary to divide an angle. This can be done in two ways: with a protractor or with a pair of compasses. To use a protractor, place it on the angle to be divided, read off a point at half of the degrees of the total angle, mark the division and draw in a line through the angle apex and this mark. To use a compass, place the point of the compass on the angle apex and mark the same arc off on both arms of the angle, place the compass point on these arcs in turn and mark off two equal arcs that cross one another within the angle; a line that is drawn through the angle apex and this cross divides the angle exactly.

Making templates

Cut out the pattern pieces from the card drawing. These pieces are called templates and will be used to cut out all your fabric pieces. It is only necessary to cut one of each shape and size. Remember that these templates do not include a seam allowance. I am very cautious and cut out extra templates adding an accurate ¼in (6mm) seam allowance all around, which enables me to cut out and sew together the fabric pieces more accurately. On some blocks it is easier to use this type of template because the templates taper into nothing and it is therefore difficult to judge the accurate size. This can be seen in the block *Winding Ways* (p. 64).

Sometimes it is necessary to see exactly which piece of fabric you are cutting out; for example, there may be a particular flower that you require in the centre of a piece. To cut this out accurately you need a window template. Make a template with the seam allowance and cut away the centre leaving the seam allowance only. When this is placed on the fabric, you can see the design and draw around the edge to get exactly the fabric piece you require.

Always label all your templates, as it is easy to muddle up a triangle from one block with a triangle from another block. If you have twenty-five blocks you are likely to have over a hundred different shaped pieces. Keep the templates from each block separate from each other. Plastic pockets are ideal for this purpose, as you can then easily find a particular template when required.

Some quiltmakers find they prefer to make their templates from more durable material. You can buy plastic sheeting which is the right thickness for cutting and is easily drawn on. It is usually available from patchwork and quilting suppliers. Plastic templates are tougher than those made from card and are not damaged by the pencil running around the edge all the time. If you intend to use your templates more than once it may be worth cutting them out in plastic.

8 A *plan of the twenty-five blocks that are constructed in this book*

Templates tend to slip when placed on the fabric. To prevent this, keep the templates steady by sticking a small piece of sandpaper on the reverse side of the template, or place a large piece of sandpaper under the fabric.

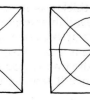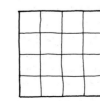

9 The basic structures on which the blocks in this book are drawn

15

Marking and cutting out the fabric pieces

Place the template on the fabric and draw around it using a soft pencil. If the pencil mark does not show up on the fabric, use a coloured pencil that will. Do not use ballpoint pens or ink markers unless you are sure they will not spoil the fabric. Experiment with any marker before marking the pieces. Keep one side of the template parallel with the grain of the fabric if possible, although you may not be able to do this if you want to select a special part of the fabric for a particular piece. Cut the pieces out and pin them to a board, arranging them in the design of the block. This keeps the pieces organized and means that you always have the appearance of the block in front of you. Cut out the borders for the block; you will need two short borders and two long ones.

Sewing the pieces into a block

Join two pieces together by placing them face to face and sewing along the seam line, making sure that you have the two seams aligned exactly. Press the seam with an iron. Some quiltmakers like to open out their seams, while others will press them to one side. I press my seams open because I find that the seams of the more complicated blocks can be very bulky and difficult to quilt through: opening out the seams spreads this bulk.

Think out the order in which you will sew the pieces together so that you do not have any corners to sew around. If you find that there are corners, I suggest you add an extra seam to eliminate them. The order of sewing is best thought out at the drawing-up stage. Later in the book you will find diagrams with the individual blocks to help you with the order of sewing. When you have sewn the block together, check its size. Blocks may vary in size, but an adjustment can be made to the block border at this stage. Sew on the block borders, first the short ones on opposite sides and then the long ones.

Curved seams are not the easiest to sew together. Pin both ends of the seam together first, then the centre and then intervals between, easing the convex curve to fit the concave one. This is a manipulative job, so take your time. Tack carefully exactly on the seam and then stitch it. Sometimes you will have to clip the convex curve to make it fit, but do not do this unless it is absolutely necessary.

Appliqué

Some of the blocks included here are assembled using appliqué. These will need a backing square of fabric the size of your block plus turnings. Structure lines can be folded or drawn on to the square and templates cut to the required shape. Fabric pieces are cut from these 1/8in (4mm) larger to allow for turning under a shallow hem. The pieces are pinned, tacked 1/4in (6mm) away from the edge and hemmed down, turning under the edge with the needle as you go and making as small a stitch as possible. A matching thread will help to make your stitching invisible. This is, however, only one of many methods of appliqué: use whichever one suits you best. In Broderie Perse the shapes are cut from an actual printed fabric and then applied to the backing fabric. Hawaiian is an appliqué cut out and applied in one piece, using a special way of folding both the fabric to be applied and the backing fabric. This method is described under the section *Hearts* (p. 44).

Log-cabin patchwork

Log-cabin is the name of a traditional block found in old quilts from both Britain and America. It is constructed from strips of fabric sewn around a central square, with dark and light strips in opposite corners. The technique of sewing these is a useful one to use when sewing any strips. Sometimes the strips are sewn to a background fabric to keep them stable.

A strip is placed face to face with and along the edge of the piece to which it is to be sewn, and then sewn along this edge through the two strips and the backing fabric (if used). The strip is then turned face up. In the log-cabin square the strips are sewn systematically round and round the centre square until the block is completed. This technique of sewing the strips is used in the *Medallion* block (p. 36).

Random patchwork

Random patchwork is a type of crazy patchwork. Pieces of fabric are sewn on to a backing fabric, adding pieces as in the sewing of strips when using the Log-cabin technique, except that in this case the pieces are irregular in shape and the straight seams are at odd angles. This form of crazy patchwork has a character of its own derived from its straight seams, unlike traditional crazy patchwork, which is a miscellany of odd shapes applied one next to the other, which quite often results in a group of ugly shapes assembled haphazardly. Random patchwork has been suggested for use in the block *Rocky Road* (p. 42).

10 A small sampler quilt with 6in square blocks. Some of the blocks have been
simplified to make it possible to complete the piecing. Quilt made by the author

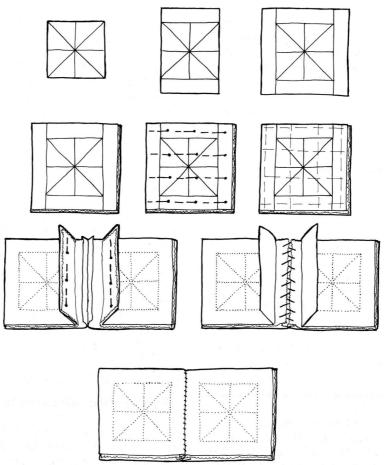

11 The 'quilt-as-you-go' method of piecing the block, bordering the block, assembling the quilt sandwich and joining the blocks together

Seminole patchwork

Seminole patchwork is a form of patchwork developed by the Seminole Indians of Florida to create an abundance of small intricate patterns. A sewing machine is used to sew together long strips of brightly coloured fabrics. These combined strips are then cut through, rearranged and sewn into patterns.

This is a time-saving technique that can be adapted and used to advantage in several traditional blocks. In this book the technique has been suggested for use in *Spider's Web* (p. 24), *Stonemason's Puzzle* (p.62), and *Goose in the Pond* (p. 74).

'Quilt-as-you-go'

This technique, as the name suggests, is a method of finishing small areas of the quilt and joining them together at a final stage. The quilt sandwich can be assembled once you have completed the piecing of a block and sewn on its borders. Cut out a piece of backing fabric and a piece of interlining, both a fraction larger than the block plus its borders. Make these into a sandwich by placing one on top of the other on a flat surface (backing, interlining, and bordered block). Pin together through all three layers, always working in one direction, and tack across, first horizontally and then vertically. The tacking needs to be sufficient to hold the three layers together in all circumstances. The quilt sandwich will be pulled in all directions if a frame is not being used. It is now ready to quilt.

Quilt the block in any way that suits the design. Ideas and suggestions are given later in the book with the individual block designs. Keep the quilting to the block at this stage. The borders are quilted once the blocks have been joined together.

To join two blocks, first pin the backing and the interlining away from the front border. Place two blocks like this face to face and sew together a border from each block. Press the seam, being careful not to harm any man-made wadding. Trim the interlinings so that they butt up to one another, and ladder stitch them together. Lay down one of the backing fabrics with the other one on top to form a hem. Stitch the hem. The borders between the blocks can now be quilted. Follow the drawings to make the method clearer.

Join all the blocks together in this way in a logical order, quilting as you go. It is not necessary to sew around any corners.

A border for the quilt can be pieced and made up into a quilt sandwich, then joined on to the quilt using the same method as for joining the blocks.

Quilting

To start quilting, first decide what colour thread you will use. A contrasting coloured thread will show up every little stitch and will to a certain extent detract from the shadow effect of your quilting. A self-toning thread will emphasize the undulating surface created by your stitching. Choose a type of thread that will easily pass through the layers of fabric and interlining. A firm crochet cotton will give you a large stitch and a 50 sewing thread will enable you to produce a small, neat stitch. Some threads will need waxing as you quilt, while others will already have a smooth surface. There are a number of these already on the market at the specialist quilting shops. Some of these threads have a polyester content and will need a little more controlling than a pure natural fibre thread. Choose a needle that you are familiar with and like using. I expect you will change your ideas on which needle to use after you have been quilting a little while. The thinner and shorter the needle, the smaller you will be able to make your quilting stitch. The thickness of the thread and the quilt sandwich will also help to determine the size of the stitch.

Take a thread 10in (25cm) to 12in (30cm) long, make a single knot in the end and thread the needle. Put the needle into the middle of the sandwich, burying the knot in the interlining and bringing the needle up where you want to begin the quilting. Take one or more stitches on to the needle through the thickness of the sandwich and pull the thread through. Continue in this way until the thread is used up and then make a knot in the thread near to the fabric surface and take it through into the middle of the sandwich and trim off the end of the thread. Complete the quilting.

There is probably no need to mark the quilting lines on the top because there are the patchwork lines to follow and cross. If marking is necessary, experiment with different ways of marking your fabric, as no two fabrics are the same. Try scratching the surface with a needle to give a bruised line, and then try a lead or a coloured pencil. Pencil marks will rub away as you quilt. Be a little more cautious with coloured pencils, because some are made from strong pigments and may stain the fabric. Some quiltmakers use with success special pens advertised especially for the job, but I have seen some disasters, so make a trial first. A way of not marking the surface of the fabric but still having a guide is to tack to the top a piece of paper or Vilene cut to the shape of the quilting pattern, and to quilt round the edge of it.

Knotting

The quilt sandwich may be secured together with a series of knots. This is a method used for joining layers together quickly or joining a thick quilt sandwich together. The sandwich must be knotted at regular intervals to hold the three layers together. The knot consists of a stitch followed by a second stitch on the same spot, the ends of which are tied in a reef knot. Traditionally the ends of the knot are left showing, but many people prefer to hide them back in the wadding.

Finishing the edge of the quilt

The edge of the quilt can be finished in whichever way you prefer. I often leave the decision about the edge until the rest of the quilt is finished, because it is then usually obvious how it needs to be done. The edge may be bound with a straight or bias binding, the front may be turned over on the back or the reverse, or turned round the interlining and the backing turned under to match and then hemmed in place.

Machine or hand sewing

Many people think that patchwork should be done by hand. This is an old-fashioned idea and is purely a preference of the maker. There are many good sewing machines on the market which help many a quiltmaker to complete a quilt that would otherwise never be finished. If you never top stitch with your machine then only an expert will know that you have used one. On the other hand, there are those who have plenty of time and do not wish to hurry making a quilt, and there is no reason why a whole quilt should not be sewn by hand. I use a machine to construct a quilt because it helps me to produce work that is precise and to tackle a task quickly and efficiently before my interest in the idea wanes. Some techniques, however, are always best done by hand.

The Blocks

The blocks in this book have been chosen from traditional British and American quilts. Their names are interesting and give hints of their derivation. Why, for example, is *Lady of the Lake* also known as *Double Sawtooth*? Individuals often change the names of blocks, perhaps naming them after a friend or a place. The log-cabin version in this book is named *Medallion* because its technique resembles the making of a medallion quilt. I do not know anyone else who calls it that: perhaps this is establishing a name that will go on into history.

These blocks have been developed during my own and my students' work to suit particular needs such as a colour scheme or shape combinations. Slight changes from the traditional idea are what create an individual design, so do not be afraid to take blocks from this book and adapt them again to suit yourself. Make the blocks do what you require from them, by changing the colour relationships and adding or taking away shapes by introducing or omitting seam lines. There are many hundreds of potential ideas in the traditional blocks, of which only a few are represented in this book. Included here are geometric blocks, appliquéd blocks, illusionary blocks and representational blocks. Books in the section on further reading include more traditional blocks.

The easiest blocks to start sewing are the geometric ones. These contain only straight lines, for example *Bear's Paw*. They are simple to draw up and do not usually require a vast range of colours or complicated sewing. The most complicated aspect is the number of pieces in a block. It is a good idea to be systematic in the way you work. One way to keep the block in order is to pin the fabric pieces to a board as you cut them out, arranged in the final layout. When you take them off the board to sew or iron a seam, replace them straight away and continue to do this until the block is completely sewn together. It is very easy to sew the wrong pieces together if they are floating all over the work table.

Each block given here will have a basic plan including all the necessary seams, how to draw it up by using its basic

12 Lady of the Lake

13 Bear's Paw

14 Medallion

grid or shape, colour suggestions, drawings of possible quilting lines, and related blocks in shape and ideas. When the block is completed its border can be added immediately, the sandwich assembled and the block quilted.

It is useful to make templates for the block border, which can be used for all the blocks. You will need two templates, a short one for the side of the block and a longer one for the side plus borders. Refer to your original quilt plan for sizes.

15 Blocks from a sampler quilt which has its own unique colour scheme made
by Deborah Khan

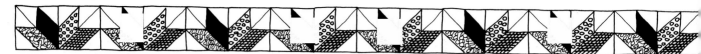

16 The Friendship Knot

 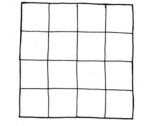 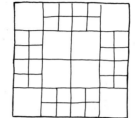 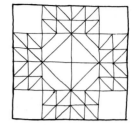 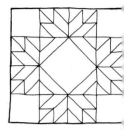

17a *The stages of drawing* The Friendship Knot

Friendship Knot

The *Friendship Knot* block is based on a four by four grid with some of the squares subdivided into a two by two grid. Draw the square of your block to the correct size, mark in the four by four grid and make the subdivisions in the right places. Now you have the necessary lines to complete the the drawing of the block. Cut out the templates and then the fabric pieces, remembering to add a seam allowance. Sew the block together in the order shown in the diagram.

The rhomboid shapes in this block can easily be cut out the wrong way round or sewn together incorrectly. They are mirror images of one another. Asymmetrical shapes need care. It helps to cut templates for both shapes and mark them clearly to remind you that although they are the same shape, in the block they appear the opposite way round to one another.

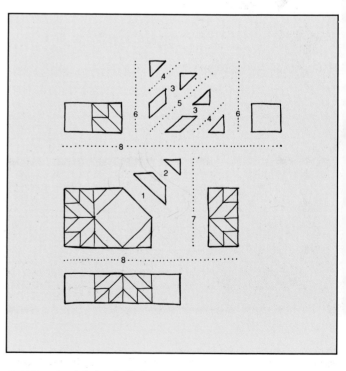

17b *The order of piecing the block*

18 Rows 1–3: *Colour and quilting ideas for* The Friendship Knot. *Row 4 top to bottom seam version of the knot,* Blazing Star, Many Pointed Star *and* Devil's Claw *or* Bright Star *on the far right*

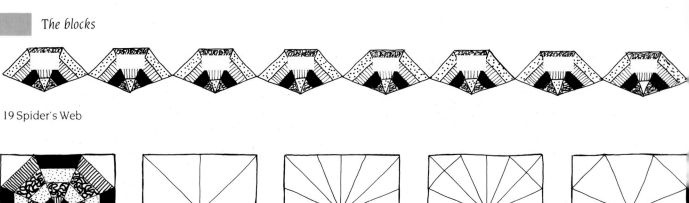

19 Spider's Web

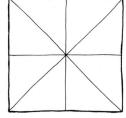
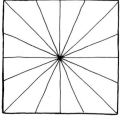
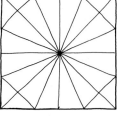
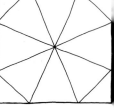

20a *The stages of drawing* Spider's Web

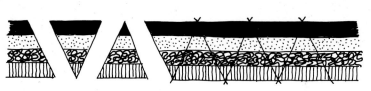

20b A *length of sewn fabric strips from which the large triangles are cut*

Spider's Web

The *Spider's Web* block is based on an octagon divided into triangles made up from strips of fabric. Draw the square of your block and then draw in the quarters and the diagonals. Divide the angles at the centre, between the diagonals and the quarters, using a protractor or a pair of compasses. To make the octagon, join the points where these lines cross the edge of the block. Erase the diagonal and quarter lines to leave eight large triangles and four smaller corner triangles. It is useful to mark the strips on the template to act as a guide when cutting out the fabric. Cut out the templates. Make a length from long strips of chosen fabrics. This should be sufficiently long and wide to cut out eight of the large triangles. Cut the large triangles from this length of strip patchwork as illustrated, and the corner triangles from a suitable fabric. Sew the triangles of the block together in the order indicated in the diagram.

You can vary the look of the block considerably by different arrangements of the strips. An even number of equal width strips will assemble to give an unmatching arrangement, and an odd number will make the middle strip run on with itself. Experiment with assembling the strips in various combinations of even and uneven widths and different colours and tonal values.

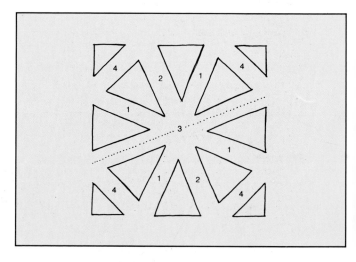

20c The *order of piecing the block*

The idea of making up a patchwork of long strips and cutting out larger shapes from it can be worked with other blocks like *Broken Dishes* or *Windmill*, both of which are made up from larger pieces. Also, you could make up your own simple block to use in this way. Some suggestions are illustrated here.

24

21 *Colour and quilting ideas, with variations of the web named* Cobweb
(4*a*), Kaleidoscope (4*b*), Merry-go-round (4*c*) *and* Windmill (4*d*) *on
the far right*

22 Spider's Web *block by Elizabeth Rowe*

23 Rose of Sharon *block by* Joan Fogg

24 Rose of Sharon

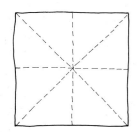

25a The stages of drawing Rose of Sharon

Rose of Sharon

The *Rose of Sharon* is a appliquéd block based on the intersections of the square. The central rose traditionally has four leaf sprays on the diagonals and four buds on the quarters of the square. There are variations of this block, and the name differs according to the reason for putting the quilt together. One variation, *Whig Rose*, appears in the coloured illustration. The emphasis is on the rose with its large petals. The buds or small flowers are much less significant. The block is certainly meant to be eye-catching.

Draw the square of your block to the correct size and mark its diagonals and quarters. Make yourself templates for the rose, the buds and the leaves. Use those drawn here as a guide, or look at the Rose of Sharon (*Hypericum calycinum*), commonly called St John's Wort, often found rampaging over gardens. Draw around the templates placing them in a pleasing arrangement to complete the design.

Use the templates to cut the fabric pieces for the flower, buds and leaves, and cut strips of fabric for the stalks. The stalks can be cut as bias strips or to shape. All the pieces need to be cut ⅛in (4mm) larger to allow for the shallow appliqué hem. Cut a fabric square the size of the block plus turnings for the back. Place the pieces on the backing square. The stalks should be applied first, then the leaves, the buds and finally the flower. If you fold and iron in the diagonals and quarters on the backing square you can use this as a guide for placing down the pieces. Pin, tack and apply the pieces to the backing square.

An alternative approach is to look for printed roses and sprays of leaves to make up your design in the Broderie Perse tradition. A little extra stuffing added to the rose

25b A rose from which ideas of shape may be taken

petals or an odd bead to accentuate the stamens could make your block look quite individual.

The leaves and stalks can be cut out in one piece, but this tends to make the design look very static. Individually cut leaves give the opportunity to angle the leaves and buds slightly to make a more realistic plant. Stalks cut from fabric on the bias give a natural looking curve. Good curved stalks can be found in many American *Whig Rose* quilts.

26 *Variations of the* Rose of Sharon *with the* Whig Rose *in the top right*

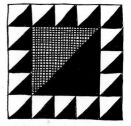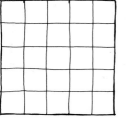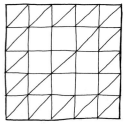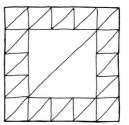

27 Lady of the Lake

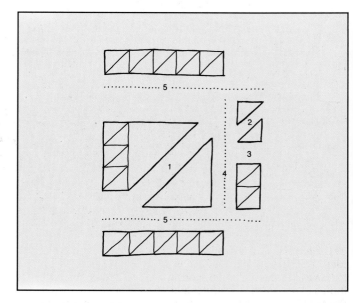

28a *The stages of drawing* Lady of the Lake

Lady of the Lake, or Double Sawtooth

The *Lady of the Lake* block is based on a five by five grid; a square surrounded by triangles. The design of the block can vary greatly with use of colour. Draw a square the size of the block and divide it into a five by five grid. Draw in the diagonals of the small squares around the edge and the large central square. Remove the unwanted grid from the centre. Make your templates, cut out your fabric pieces and join them together in the logical order indicated in the diagram.

The large triangles in the centre can be sub-divided by quilting or the space can be filled with some larger and perhaps representational quilted design, or with a large print fabric which can be quilted around.

There are a large number of blocks that use triangles in their design, and many refer to birds in their names. Some are illustrated here. It is easy to understand that the triangle represents a bird or an aeroplane and a group of triangles a flock; and that the jagged edge made by the triangles in this block has the name Sawtooth.

28b *The order of piecing the block*

29 *Quilting ideas and variations of the* Lady of the Lake *along with* Flock (6b), Ann and Andy (5c), Dutchman's Puzzle (6c), Aircraft (4d), Anvil (5d), Wild Goose Chase (6d), Northwind (3e), Birds in Air (4e), Indian Plume (5e), Flying Dutchman (6e), Flying Birds (2f), Sail Boat (3f), Winged Square (4f), Hovering Hawks (5f) *and* Sparrows' Garden (6f)

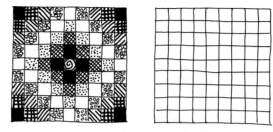

30 Trip around the World

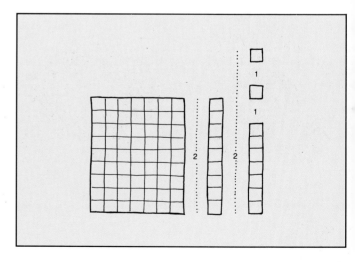

31a *The drawing of the* Trip around the World

Trip around the World

Trip around the World is the name given to a quilt design made up of squares where colours revolve round the centre square. It can be used with success to create many varying appearances. It gives an opportunity to play with fabrics and to find out how they react together. You can use them to juxtapose and contrast with one another, or to relate to one another. It gives an opportunity to create a mood because you are able to use a greater variety of fabrics than in some of the other blocks. Base your block on an odd numbered grid to give a centre square. The size of the square that your grid gives will no doubt dictate the actual grid used. Relate the size to the shapes in the other blocks. Draw up the square and make a template. Cut out your fabrics. Join them together systematically. I lay out the pieces in the pattern of the block, sew the squares together in strips, then sew the strips together to form the block.

31b *The order of piecing the block*

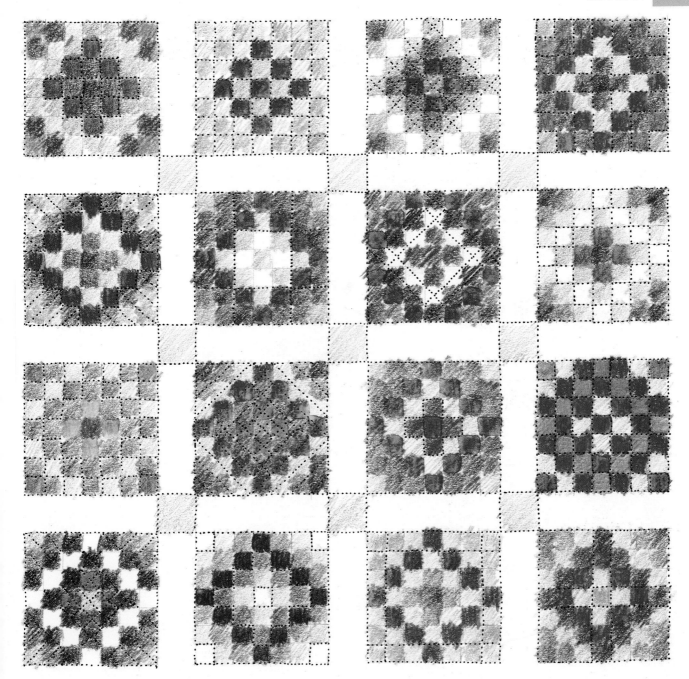

32 *Colour suggestions for the* Trip around the World

33 Trip around the World *by Pat Salt*

34 Medallion *block by the author*

35 Medallion

Medallion

The aim of the *Medallion* block is to give the appearance of one square floating on top of another, and it is derived from the *Log-cabin* block. Draw the square of your block to the correct size and mark off the half-way points on the sides of the square. Join these points to make a square. These are the basic shapes of the block which are to be filled with strips using the log-cabin technique. Cut out the templates. Use the templates to cut out pieces in a backing fabric, not forgetting the seam allowances. Mark with a fold the diagonals of the square piece and the half of the triangular pieces, and pin the small square and small triangles in position as shown in the diagram. Apply log-cabin strips to these shapes using the techniques described on p. 16. Keep one fabric to one round of the patchwork of the square, and keep the four triangles exactly the same. The width of strips will contribute to the character of the block. The narrower the strips, the greater the variety of fabrics used, which gives greater scope for adjusting the mood of the block. When the patchwork is finished, join the square and triangles together as indicated in the diagram.

Emphasize the floating square by using contrasting tones or colours for the square and triangles. A cold colour, such as blue, will recede, and a warm colour, such as red, will advance. A change in tone from the square to the triangles will also make one come forward and the other go

 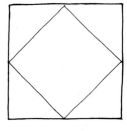

36a The stages of drawing the Medallion

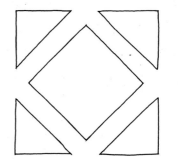 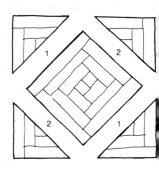

36b The order of piecing the block

back. Experiment with mixing the colours and tones to find other combinations that move away from one another, and perhaps rearrange the tonal balance of the square to the triangles.

36c The application of the log-cabin method of sewing the strips of fabric round the triangle

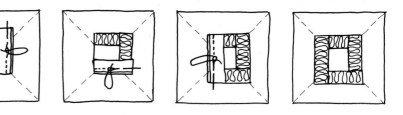

36d The log-cabin method of sewing the strips of fabric round the square

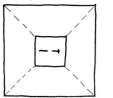 

37 Medallion *blocks showing how light and dark arrangements of the*
sections of the block can make variations on the original idea

38 Card Trick

 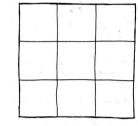 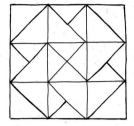

39a *The stages of drawing* Card Trick

Card Trick

The *Card Trick* block derives its name from its resemblance to four cards placed one behind the other. It is based on a three by three grid. Draw the block to size. Draw in the diagonals of the triangles where shown in the diagram. Cut out the templates and use them to cut out the fabric pieces. Sew the pieces together in the order indicated.

The illusion of this block is created by using the same or similar fabrics for the triangles that make one card. Use light-toned fabrics against dark-toned fabrics, contrasting coloured fabrics against each other, or unusual fabrics that have a decorative stripe, and carefully cut out the triangles so that the designs go round the cards. This emphasizes the design. When using stripes it is helpful to mark the direction of the stripe on the template.

There are several more blocks illustrated here that can give a three-dimensional idea. Experiment with them, using at least three tones of fabric to create the illusion.

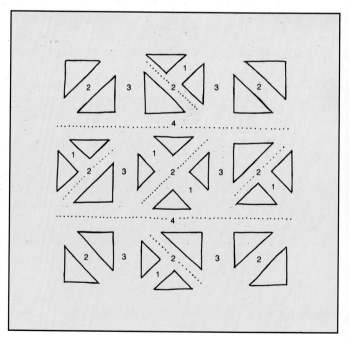

39b *The order of piecing the block*

40 *Row a and 1 b Five Card Trick blocks. Other blocks that can be made to give an illusion of space:* Brown Goose (2*b*), Bachelor's Puzzle (3*b*), Interlocking Squares (4*b*), Honeycomb (1*c*), Woven Star (2*c*), Jennifer's Star (3*c*), Attic Windows (4*c*), Building Blocks (1*d*), Jack in the Box (2*d*), Patchwork Star (3*d*) *and* Nelson's Star (4*d*) *reading from the second block in the second row*

41 Note the use of striped fabric to go round the cards in the Card Trick block
by the author

42 Rocky Road *block by Margot Stonestreet*

43 Rocky Road

 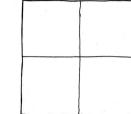 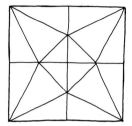

44a The stages of drawing Rocky Road

Rocky Road

The *Rocky Road* block is a simple one, containing only sixteen pieces. Draw the block to size and quarter it. Take a point on the quarter lines equidistant from the centre. Join these points to make a square. Complete the drawing by putting in the lines from the corners to the points on the quarter lines. The shapes of this block will vary considerably, depending on where you place the points on the quarter lines. Choose those shapes which give you angles that you can manage easily in the sewing stage. Some of the blocks have less acute angles. Cut out the templates.

It is possible to work random patchwork, as described in the techniques section, on the large pieces of this simple block. Make a piece of random patchwork sufficiently large to cut out the four triangles. Make a window template of the triangles so that you can choose exactly the piece of patchwork to cut out. It will make the sewing easier if larger seam allowances are used for this block to provide for the extra bulk made by the random patchwork. Cut out the fabric pieces and sew the block together in the order illustrated. The pieces will be of different thickness, so let the seam allowances turn in their own direction.

There are many traditional blocks with the same simplicity as *Rocky Road*, and which can be used in a similar way with some form of patchwork making up the larger pieces. A few of these blocks are illustrated here. To use random or crazy patchwork like this contains its natural tendency to become out of control.

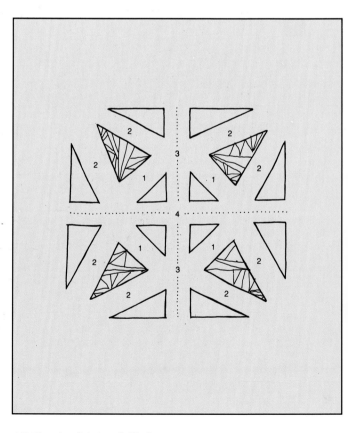

44b The order of piecing the block

45 Rocky Road (*top right*) *and* Bow Tie (*bottom left*) *illustrating where to use random patchwork along with the outline shapes of* Watermill (1*a*), Broken Dishes (2*a*), Churn Dash (1*b*), Washington's Puzzle (2*b*), Variable Star (1*c*), Double Pinwheel (2*c*), Patience's Corner (3*d*), Tea Leaf (4*d*), Birds in Air (5*d*), Nine Patch (3*e*), Windmill (4*c*) *and* Nelson's Victory (5*e*), *all of which can be used in the same way*

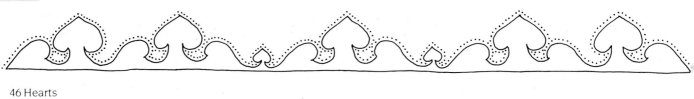

46 Hearts

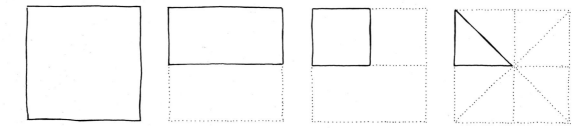

47a The folding of the paper and fabric for Hawaiian appliqué

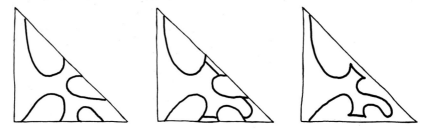

Hearts

47b The stages of drawing the Hearts block on the folded paper

The *Hearts* block is assembled using the Hawaiian method of applying a one-piece fabric cut-out to a background fabric. It is designed in the same way as those snowflake cut-outs that children make in infant school. To design your block, use the folded paper cut-out method. Take a piece of lightweight paper, such as greaseproof or lay-out paper, the size of your block folded into eighths as shown in the diagram. Draw four half hearts on the folds. Join these together to make a continuous line as shown in the diagram. Cut along this line through all the layers of paper. Unfold the paper to reveal your design. Redraw and cut until you are satisfied with the shape of the cut-out. Cut out an eighth of this design to be your template and remake in card for strength.

Take a backing square plus turnings and fold it into eighths as directed in the diagram for folding the paper. Iron the folds in well. Take a square of the fabric that you wish to apply in the size of the block and fold it in exactly the same way as you have the backing fabric. You must start folding both fabrics right side upwards. Place the template on the top of the folded appliqué fabric and draw around it. Cut it out, leaving ⅛in (4mm) extra fabric allowance for turning the hem. Unfold the backing square and place it face up on the table. Place the folded appliqué fabric on the backing square in the correct eighth. Now

47c The Hearts *shape showing the eighth section from which the template is made*

48 Variations on the idea of Hearts

unfold it matching fold with fold of both pieces of fabric. If these folds match, the two pieces will keep easily in place. Pin and tack the appliqué fabric to the backing square ¼in (8mm) away from the edge of the design. Match the sewing thread with the appliqué fabric and apply to the backing square. The work easily folds up in these same folds between working sessions.

Traditional Hawaiian appliqué is usually made up in plain coloured fabrics. To make an individual block, choose an unusual patterned fabric and try designing your own cut-outs. There are some more ideas here based on traditional cut-outs.

45

49 Hearts *block by the author*

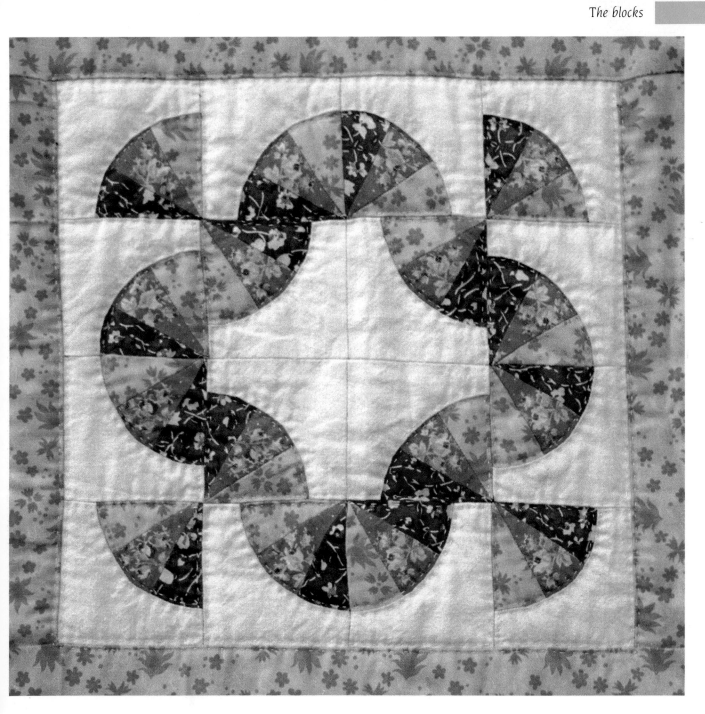

50 Mohawk Trail *block by Pat Salt*

51 Mohawk Trail

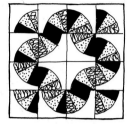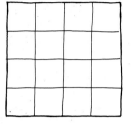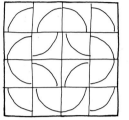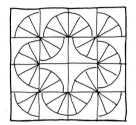

52a The stages of drawing Mohawk Trail

Mohawk Trail

The *Mohawk Trail* block is based on a simple square, turned and placed in a four by four grid. Draw up the square of your block and divide it into a four by four grid. In a corner of each small square draw an arc with the compass point on the intersections of the squares. These arcs should all be the same size. Be sure not to leave the sides to which the arcs come too small, as this will make sewing the block difficult. Using a protractor, divide the arc into as many sections as you like. Make the templates and cut out the fabric pieces. Assemble the small squares as indicated in the diagram, then sew them together, without sewing around a corner, to complete the block.

The name of this block may come from its resemblance in shape to the hatchet of the Mohawk Indians; or the name could have come from the Mohawk trail winding through the Appalachian hills. I see the shape, with the fan shapes surrounding the centre, as reminiscent of a formal English garden. If you think of it in this way, you could relate the colours to flowers and the quilting to paths. Experiment with different arrangements of the small squares to design your own block.

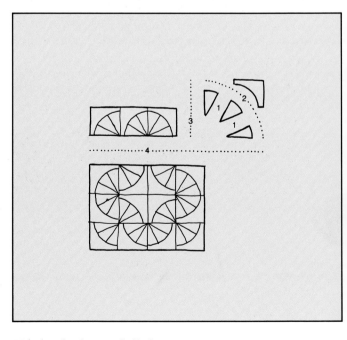

52b The order of piecing the block

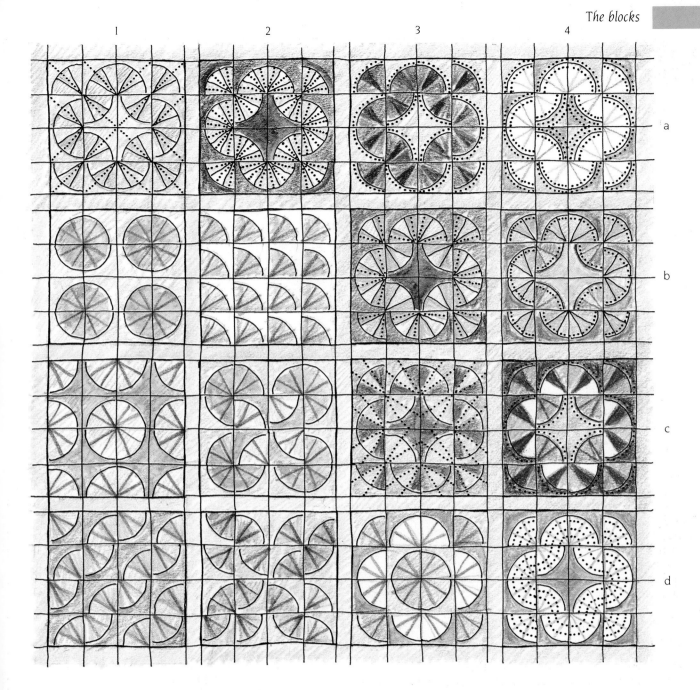

53 *Nine versions of the* Mohawk Trail *along with different arrangements of
the small squares to make* Plates (1*b*), Fans (2*b*), Millwheel (1*c*),
Wonder of the World (2*c*), Falling Trees (1*d*), Drunkard's Path (2*d*)
and Love Ring (3*d*), *reading from the second row*

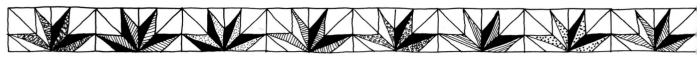

54 Star

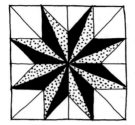 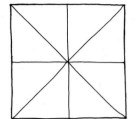 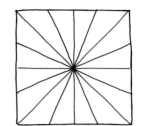 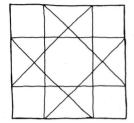 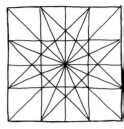

55a The stages of drawing the Star

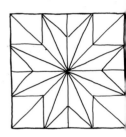

Star

There must be more star designs than any others in patchwork, and there are many more star designs still to be thought out. They can be simple or complex in construction. The star blocks here are based on an eight-pointed star and drawn on an octagon. Draw the square of your block to size, then draw in the diagonals and quarters of the block. Divide all the angles at the centre to give the eight points of your star on the edge of the block. For the moment ignore all the lines through the centre. Join the eight points to those directly opposite, straight and diagonally across the square. This makes a star. The lines through the centre can now help you to design the middle of the star. Erase those lines not needed. Cut out the templates and fabric pieces. Sew the pieces together in the order shown in the diagram, arranging the seams neatly on the back where the sixteen come together in the centre.

This is an attractive design but it does present the difficulty of sewing the sixteen pieces together at the centre. Use the lines in the drawing to design your own star. There are some suggestions for you here. Choose for the star colours that emphasize the shape.

55b The order of piecing the block

56 *Variations of the* Eight-Pointed Star

57 Four Baskets

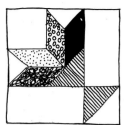
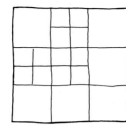
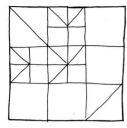
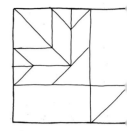
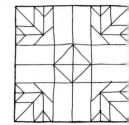

58a *The stages of drawing the* Basket of Scraps *block and repeating it to make* Four Baskets

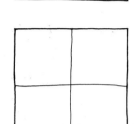

Four Baskets

Many of the traditional blocks are designed to be viewed one way up in a quilt. If you would like your quilt to be versatile and hang or lie in any direction, then there is no reason why you should not repeat one block within your block area, and so make a block that is more complex but looks satisfactory whichever way up it is placed. The *Basket of Scraps* adapts well to this approach. It is best not to use any block that is too intricate to start with, because you are inevitably making a complex block just by repeating the original one four times. Choose your block and note its grid. Draw your block square and quarter it. Draw the grid into each quarter: if you have a three by three grid, you will now have a block of six by six grid. Draw the block on the grid in each quarter, turning the block round in each quarter. Cut out the templates and the fabric pieces. Sew them together in a logical order so that you do not have to sew around any awkward corners. Try experimenting with two, or even more, different blocks, combining them into one.

The drawings here show a simple *Basket of Scraps* drawn up and multiplied four times. There are some more ideas illustrated here that you might like to try. If you feel confident, you might try varying the proportions of the chosen block and eliminating any imbalance that occurs through multiplying it.

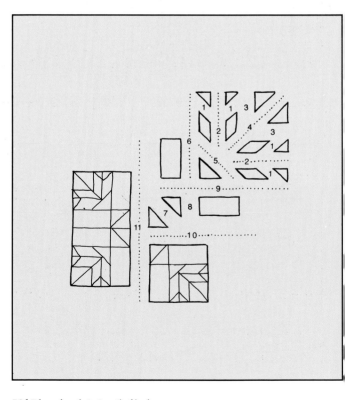

58b *The order of piecing the block*

59 *Two blocks made from* Basket of Scraps (1a *and* 3b) *and others made from* Tall Pine (2a), Palm Leaf (3a), Cactus Flower (1b), Flower Basket (2b), Hosanna (1c), House *and* Tree (3c)

60 Sunburst

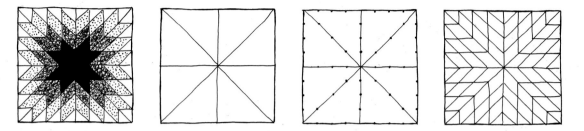

61a The stages of drawing the Sunburst

Sunburst

Sunburst is the name given to a quilt with a star of diamonds surrounded by rows and rows of more diamonds. True diamonds grouped like this do not fit into a square. To make a satisfactory block the star can be made up from rhomboids, with rows of rhomboids surrounding it. Draw the square of the block the correct size and draw in the quarters and the diagonals. Decide how many rows of rhomboids you require, and mark this number of points, equidistant on each side of all the triangles. In each triangle join the points on the side of the block with the points opposite on first one and then on the other side of the triangle, as shown in the diagram. This completes the drawing of the block. Remember that the rhomboids are not true diamonds and are mirror images of those in the neighbouring triangles. Make your templates and cut out your fabric pieces. Sew the rhomboids together with the triangle pieces as indicated in the diagram to complete the block.

The possibilities of this block are similar to those in the *Trip around the World*. Experiment with your fabrics, trying to arrange them to burst out in colour as its name suggests; dark to light or light to dark.

61b The order of piecing the block

62 Sunburst *blocks showing some of the variations to be made by varying the position of the tone or colour*

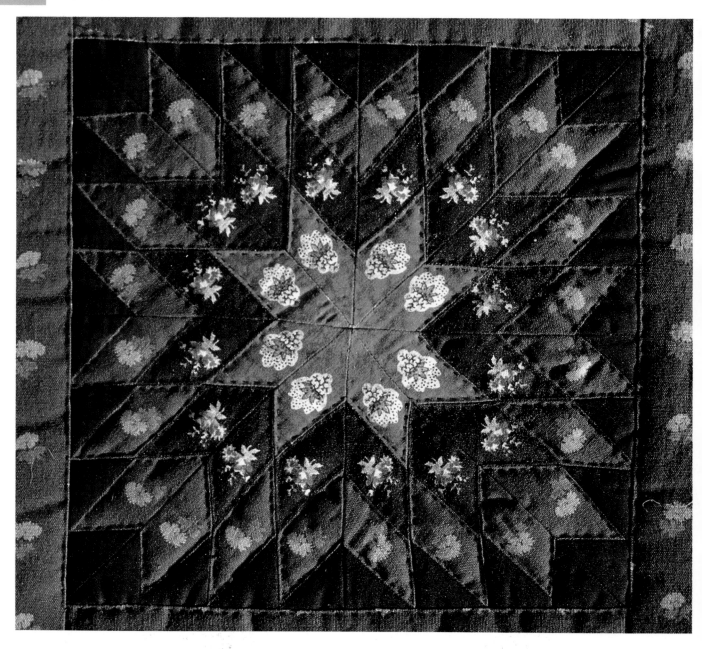

63 Note how special pieces of fabric have been selected for the rhomboids in the
Sunburst block by Pat Salt

64 Note the embroidered initials in the corner of the Mariner's Compass
block by Dorothy Elder

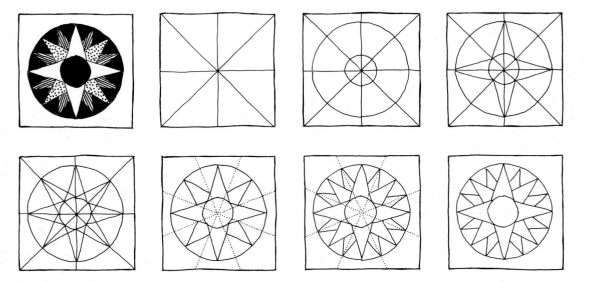

65 Mariner's Compass

66a The stages of drawing the Mariner's Compass *block*

Mariner's Compass

The *Mariner's Compass* looks a complex block to draw, but if you are careful it will all fit into place. I suggest that you use a different coloured pencil for each set of points. Be sure to keep pencil points sharp to make accurate drawings. Draw the square of your block and draw in the diagonal and quarter lines. Decide how large you want the compass and its centre to be; the smaller the centre circle, the narrower your compass points will be. I suggest you start with it not too small and be prepared to redraw it again if you dislike it. Initial in the N, E, S, and W points, and the NE, SE, SW and NW points. Join the points where the quarter lines cross the outer circle with the points where the diagonal lines cross the inner circle. You now have the N, E, S and W arms established. Join the points in the opposite way to establish the NE, SE, SW and NW points. To draw in further points of the compass, you must now draw in more lines through the centre point and the points where the arms of the already established points intersect. Using these lines and ignoring the others, join the points from the outer circle to the inner circle. You should now have sixteen points to your compass. It is possible to go on and draw in more points in the same way. Eliminate any unnecessary lines. Cut out the templates and fabric pieces and sew

66b The order of piecing the compass

them together in the order shown in the diagram. Apply the assembled compass to a square of fabric the size of your block with turnings, and trim away the extra fabric behind the points. Apply the centre of the compass in place to complete the block.

Decide which part of the compass you wish to stand out, and make the adjacent pieces contrast in tone or colour. Look at compass designs on old maps to help you design an original one. There are hundreds of variations of the compass design: enough to keep many quiltmakers designing for a lifetime.

67 Four Compasses *based on different centres to show the varying character of the block*

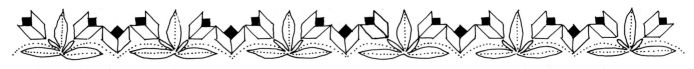

68 Tulips

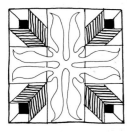
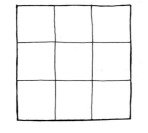
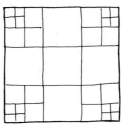
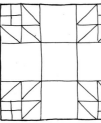
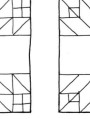
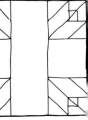

69a The stages of drawing the flower heads for the Tulips block

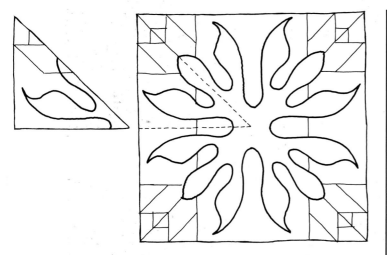

69b The drawing of the leaves on the eighth section from which the template is made

69c The order of piecing the flower heads

Tulips

The *Tulips* block is made up from a combination of piecing and appliqué techniques. The flower heads are pieced and the leaves applied. The block is based on a three by three grid: the four corner squares are sub-divided into two by two and then the small corner squares further sub-divided into two by two. Draw the square of your block and mark in the sub-divisions. You now have the necessary lines to draw in the tulip heads as shown in the diagram. Erase any lines not required. Make templates for the flower pieces. Sew the block together in the order shown. Make a template for the leaves using the Hawaiian folded method described in the section *Hearts* (p. 44) with the stem of the flower along the diagonal and a leaf growing out of it. Remember to design the leaves and stem with a continuous line from one side of the folded paper triangle to the other folded side. Fold the block and the square of fabric for the leaves into eighths. Cut out the leaves using the template. Apply the leaves to the block using the technique described for the *Hearts* block (p. 44).

There are a great number of traditional pieced flowers that can be used in this block. Look in your garden for more flower shapes and leaf shapes that complement the chosen flowers.

70 Nine different shaped flowers and leaves to vary the Tulips block

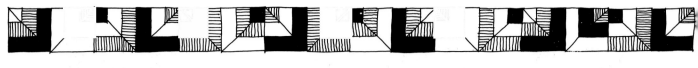

71 Stonemason's Puzzle

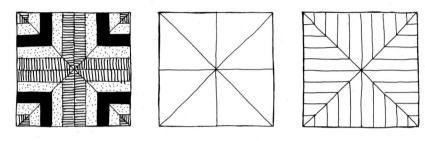

72a *The stages of drawing* Stonemason's Puzzle

72b *A length of sewn fabric strips from which the triangles are cut*

Stonemason's Puzzle

The *Stonemason's Puzzle* block, like *Spider's Web* (p. 24), is a block in which triangles can be cut out from a length of fabric strips sewn together. Draw the square of your block to size and then add the diagonals and quarters. This is all the lines that you need for the block, but it is useful to mark in the strips on the triangle to act as a guide when cutting out the fabric. The interest in this design lies in the combination of strips of fabric sewn together. The length of the sewn strips should be twice that of the side of the block plus seam allowances. Make the triangular template, sew your strips of fabric together, cut the triangles out of the sewn strips and sew them together in the order shown.

I suggest that an odd number of strips are sewn together, arranging them symmetrically to obtain a cross in the design. This broad cross lends itself to being quilted. There is no reason why you should not make other arrangements of the strips to create a different emphasis in design. This block is particularly interesting when it is repeated, with a lattice surrounding each one.

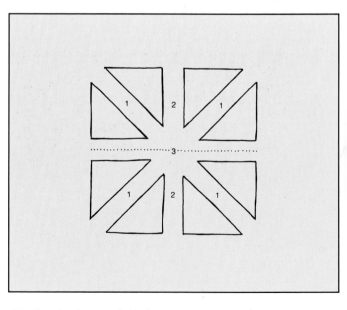

72c *The order of piecing the block*

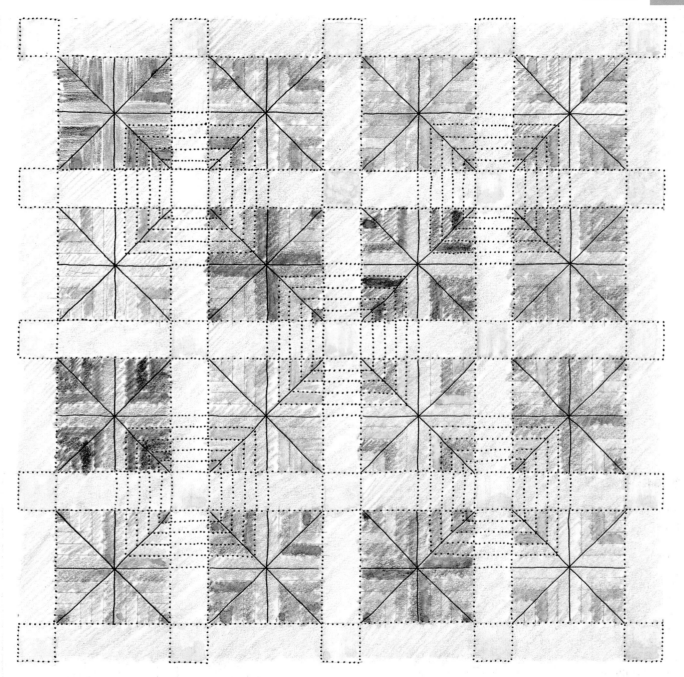

73 Stonemason's Puzzle *repeated to show how this block makes an overall design for a quilt as will many of the blocks within the book*

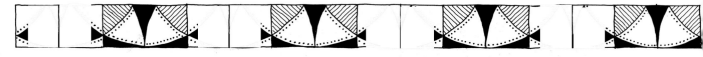

74 Winding Ways

 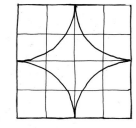 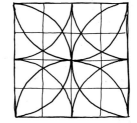 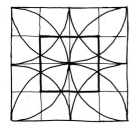 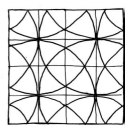

75a *The stages of drawing a quarter of the* Winding Ways *block which is then repeated for the other quarters of the block*

Winding Ways

The *Winding Ways* block is based on a series of circles which overlap to give shield-like shapes. Draw a square the size of your block and divide it with a four by four grid. Draw arcs half the length of the side of the block using the compass point on the corners of the square and then arcs with the point on the centre of the sides of the square. The centre four squares of this drawing are a quarter of the block, and one of the small squares multiplied sixteen times is the complete block. Cut out the templates, being particularly careful with the tapering shapes: it is easy to make these pieces too short. This is a case for making templates with an exact ¼in (8mm) seam allowance. The piecing of this block is fiddly. It is useful to pin through exact points and sew over the pins. Some patchworkers apply the shield shapes to eliminate working the intricate piecing, but it is not so easy to obtain the graceful curves in this way.

If you find this too difficult, try designing a different block using a pair of compasses. *Dolly Madison's Workbox* is another block with curves but it still has the tapering pieces, as do many of the curved seam blocks. Several of the simpler curved seam blocks are shown. Choose colours or tones that will show up the circular lines: it would be disappointing to lose the graphic quality in these designs.

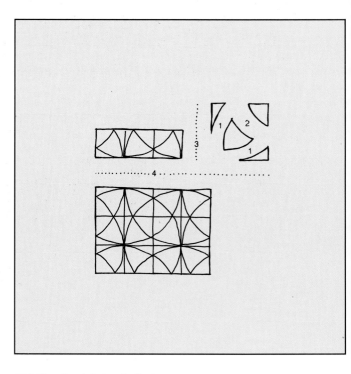

75b *The order of piecing the block*

76 *Repeats of* Winding Ways *to show the circles that make up the block along with simpler blocks below*; Dorothy Madison's Workbox (1d), Orange Peel (2d), Millwheel (3d) *and* Crossways (4d) *which are also based on a circle*

77 Monkey Wrench

 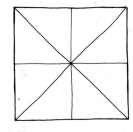 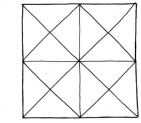 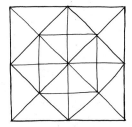 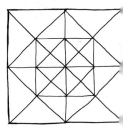

78a The stages of drawing Monkey Wrench

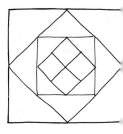

Monkey Wrench, or Indiana Puzzle

The *Monkey Wrench* is a block that creates an illusion of curves without any curved seams, by strategically placing angled seams to create this illusion. Draw the square of your block to size and mark in the quarter and diagonal lines. Join the points where the quarter lines divide the sides into a square. Join the points where the diagonal lines divide this square into another square. Go on making square within square until you think that the pieces are as small as you can manage. Erase the quarter and diagonal lines except in the centre square. Make your templates and cut out the fabric pieces, contrasting the colour of one arm of the design with the other. Join the pieces by starting in the middle of the block and following the order shown in the diagram.

Another traditional block that gives an illusion of curves is *Storm at Sea*. It is essential to have the contrast of tone or colour to emphasize the curves. Illustrated is an example of this block, and as you will see it uses a wider variety of shapes than the *Monkey Wrench*. Blocks of this kind are particularly interesting when seen in a continuous layout. Your block could be repeated four times within the block to make it look more interesting. *Storm at Sea* has a slightly different repeat, with only three quarters of the block repeated.

Blocks that are based on an octagon have undulating lines that move gently across a quilt: see *Spider's Web* (p. 24) and *Castle Wall* (p. 80).

78b The order of piecing the block

79 Monkey Wrench *design above showing how the shapes can alter by turning the block in different directions, and the* Storm at Sea *below showing the waving lines that are produced by repeating three-quarters of the block*

80 Martha Washington's Wreath

81a The stages of drawing Martha Washington's Wreath

Martha Washington's Wreath

Martha Washington's Wreath is an appliquéd block and, as its name suggests, is based on a circle. Traditionally it has four flowers, each with a bud and three leaves, all placed on the circle. There are many variations of the wreath to be found on nineteenth-century American quilts.

Draw the square of your block to the correct size with its quarter and diagonal lines. Draw a circle the size of the wreath in the centre. Many early needlewomen used household articles to help them draw their designs. A plate could be used to draw the basis of the wreath. Make templates for the flower, bud and leaf. If you have little confidence in your ability to draw a free shape, try drawing some similar to those in the drawings here, or, alternatively, draw around some actual flowers and leaves of the right size to make the templates. Keep the shapes simple and not too small (this is a mistake often made when doing appliqué work). Draw around the templates on to the circle, placing the flowers, buds and leaves exactly where you want them to complete the design of the wreath using the circle and lines as a guide.

Use the templates to cut out the fabric pieces. These pieces need to be slightly larger than the templates to allow for the shallow hem in appliqué. Cut a bias strip of fabric for the wreath, and a fabric square the size of the block plus turnings for the background. Tack the wreath in place. Place the cut fabric pieces, using your drawing as a guide, on the fabric backing square. Pin, tack and apply the pieces.

81b A wreath from which ideas of shape may be taken

The large flower prints found in English furnishing cottons are suitable for cutting out and using in the Broderie Perse method. This would give you a realistic and original block. Fill the wreath with flowers and foliage to create a florist's wreath. You will see that some of the wreaths are quite stylized and others more realistic. Design your wreath to fit in with the blocks you have already completed.

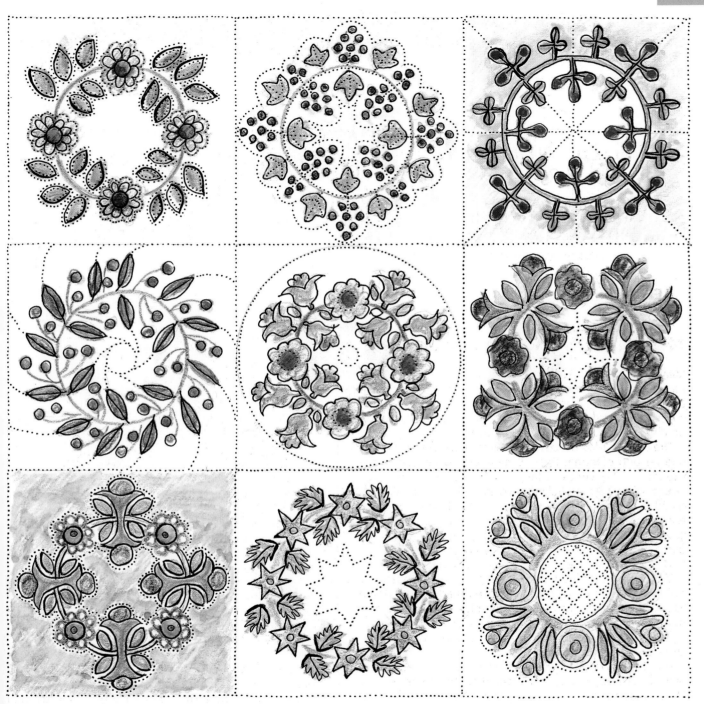

82 Wreath ideas taken from traditional American quilts

83 Note the unusual use of fabric in the Martha Washington's Wreath by
Jean Powell

84 Note the gentle change of colour in the Indian Summer Ring by Karen
MacFadyen

85 Indian Summer Ring

 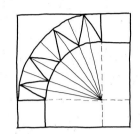 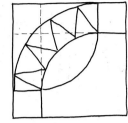 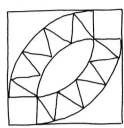 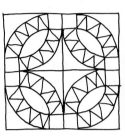

86a *The stages of drawing* Indian Summer Ring

Indian Summer Ring

The *Indian Summer Ring* block is a variation of the popular *Wedding Ring* block. You do not have to draw the complete block to obtain the templates, but the complete drawing will give you the necessary lines to judge whether you have got the proportions to your satisfaction. Draw a square a quarter the size of your block, and in two opposite corners draw a small square, each the same size. These squares will give you the width of your rings. In a third corner draw a square of the same size on which to construct the arc of the ring. With the compass point on the inner corner of the construction square, draw an arc to connect the inner corners of the other two small squares. Change the arc of the compass and draw an arc parallel to the first, joining the two outer points. With a protractor divide the right-angle made by the inner corners of the small squares into twice as many sections as you want triangles in the arc of the ring. Starting at the inner corner of one square, join the points where the divisions of the right-angle cross the ring alternately from inner to outer ring. Draw a construction

square in the fourth corner and, using this, draw the opposite arc, joining the inner corners to give the eye shape of the block. This completes the drawing of the section of the ring required for templates. Go on drawing the rest of the block, being aware of the many construction lines as you draw. It can be very muddling. Cut out the templates required. The tapering outside pieces are best made with an exact ¼in (8mm) seam allowance. Cut out the fabric pieces and sew them together in the order shown in the diagram.

This block is ideal for using up very small pieces of fabric. The triangular pieces can make pleasing additional shapes within the rings, depending on where you place the strongest tones or colour contrasts. This makes the block more interesting when used in isolated situations, as in this quilt, and the eye is distracted from the circle. The curve of this block drawing gives a squarish feel. If you do not like this, try drawing the block from the outside corner of the construction square instead of from the inside corner.

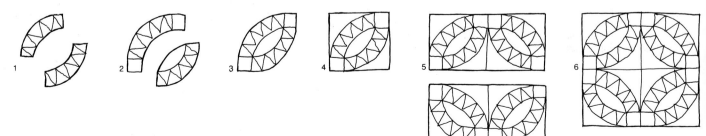

86b *The order of piecing the block*

87 Indian Summer Ring *blocks showing the different shapes made by having a different number of triangles in the arc and a* Double Wedding Ring *block bottom right*

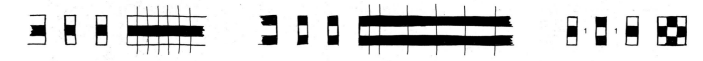

88 Goose in the Pond

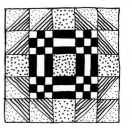 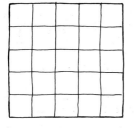 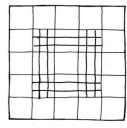 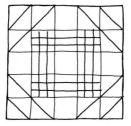

89a *The stages of drawing the* Goose in the Pond

89b *The order of cutting and piecing the small squares*

Goose in the Pond

The *Goose in the Pond* block is based on a five by five grid with some of the inner squares sub-divided into three by three. The triangles in the corners are the goose or geese, and I imagine that the smaller squares in the middle are the ripples on the pond. Draw the square of the block, the three by three sub-divisions and the triangles where shown. Cut out the templates and the fabric pieces. Sew the block together in the order shown.

To save time, it is possible to cut out and sew the pieces in the central squares using the Seminole method of piecing patterns as described in the chapter on techniques. Decide on the width of the small rectangular pieces and sew together two sets of fabric strips the width of the small rectangle plus turnings; one set with ABA fabric strips and the other with BAB. From these sets, cut out squares and small rectangles which are sewn together to make up the other squares. Do not forget the seam allowances. This may not be an economical or a quick method for assembling one block, but when you start multiplying up the number of blocks you are making then it may be helpful to streamline your cutting and sewing in this way.

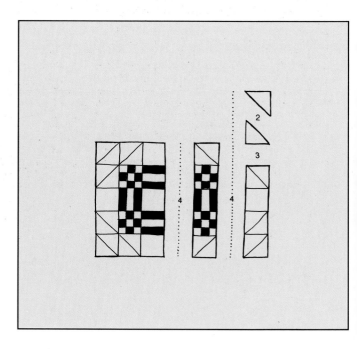

89c *The order of piecing the block*

90 *Colour and quilting ideas for* Goose in the Pond *together with* Nest and Fledgling, Handy Andy *and* Wedding Ring *along the bottom*

91 Dresden Plate

92a *The stages of drawing* Dresden Plate

Dresden Plate

The Dresden Plate block is a very old and well-known block, and a great favourite to use up odd pieces of fabric from the ragbag. It varies in its number of pieces and in its straight or scalloped outer edge.

Draw the square of the block and draw in the quarter lines. Decide on the size of your plate and draw the two circles with a pair of compasses in the centre of the square. Using a protractor, divide the centre of the plate into equal sections. To make a scalloped edge, cut yourself a curve to fit the sections, or find a round object that will fit, such as an egg-cup, and draw around it to fit into the sections and make the edge. Make the templates, cut out the fabric pieces and sew them together. First sew two sections of the rim together, then four, and so on until all the sections are joined into a circle. The outer edge is then applied to a backing square the size of the block plus turnings. The centre of this backing fabric can be trimmed away to reduce bulk. The centre circle of the plate is then applied and the block is finished. If you have made a straight edge to the plate, it is possible to sew this to the backing fabric on the machine, having first trimmed away the unwanted fabric from the centre. This will probably enable you to obtain a better curve.

Now is an ideal opportunity to look at the blocks you have completed so far, because the Dresden Plate has a large number of equal pieces where you could introduce a new fabric or colour or repeat one that has not been used very much to help the overall balance of the quilt design.

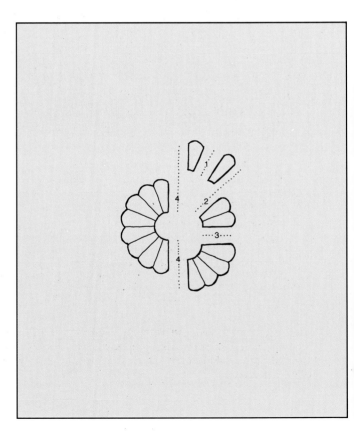

92b *The order of piecing the plate*

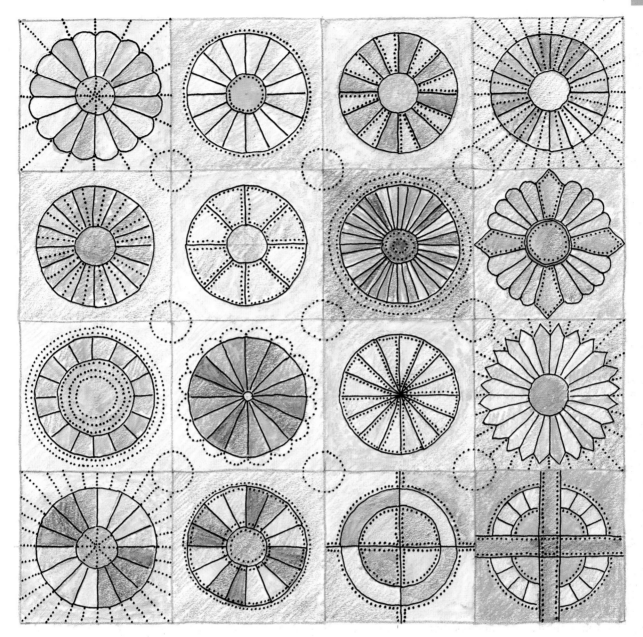

93 *Variations of the Dresden Plate showing different types of edge to the plate, varying number of sections within the plate, ideas for use of colour and tone, and two blocks also based on the circle,* Fair Play *and* Ladies' Fancy *bottom right*

94 Dresden Plate *gives the opportunity to use a large number of fabrics in one block as Pat Salt has done here*

95 Castle Wall *by Ursula Hunt*

96 Castle Wall

97a *The stages of drawing* Castle Wall

Castle Wall

The *Castle Wall* block is complex, but it is well worthwhile spending the time sorting out the maze of lines to play with the pattern of shapes. Draw the square of the block to size. Draw in the diagonals and the quarters of the block, divide all the angles at the centre and join the points where these divisions cross the edge of the block to make an octagon. Erase all internal lines. Join all the opposite points of the octagon. This gives you a small octagon in the centre. Join the opposite points of the small octagon, extending the lines across the block. You now have all the necessary points from which to complete the drawing. Follow the diagram. Erase any unnecessary lines and cut out the templates and fabric pieces. Sew the block together in the order shown in the diagram.

An imaginative way to use fabric is to cut out special parts of a pattern for particular pieces. Choose a striped pattern to go around the wall of the castle, or cut out flowers for the central triangles to make a formal garden. This way of looking at fabric gives the work a united and tidy character. It is possible to get several ideas from one fabric. Fancy striped prints or border prints are useful for sorting out gems of design to be cut out and used to transform a block in this way.

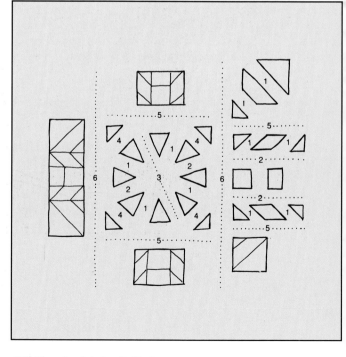

97b *The order of piecing the block*

80

1   2   3

a

b

c

98 Castle Wall *blocks which suggest the ways that striped fabrics can be used to aid the design of a block along with three blocks based on the same octagon* Broken Star (3a), Castle Keep (3b) *and* Path to Rome (3c) *on the far right*

99 Bear's Paw

100a The stages of drawing Bear's Paw

Bear's Paw

The Bear's Paw block is based on a seven by seven grid and represents the bear's four pawprints. Draw a square the size of the required block and divide it into a seven by seven grid. Draw in the lines of the block on the grid, using the diagram as a guide, and remove any lines not required. Make your templates, cut out your fabrics and sew the pieces together in the order indicated.

The appearance of the block can be quite different if you make the central cross disappear into the background and therefore emphasize the paw shapes with their claws. This can be done by choosing the same fabric for the cross as for the background edge triangles and having the paws and their claws in the same toned fabric.

There are several blocks which have a similar arrangement, with spiky triangles in various directions around the edge, not all based on the seven by seven grid. The triangles around the edge vary in arrangement and the four squares are divided up in different patterns.

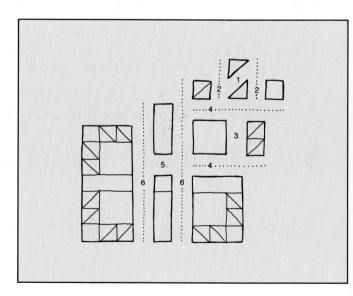

100b The order of piecing the block

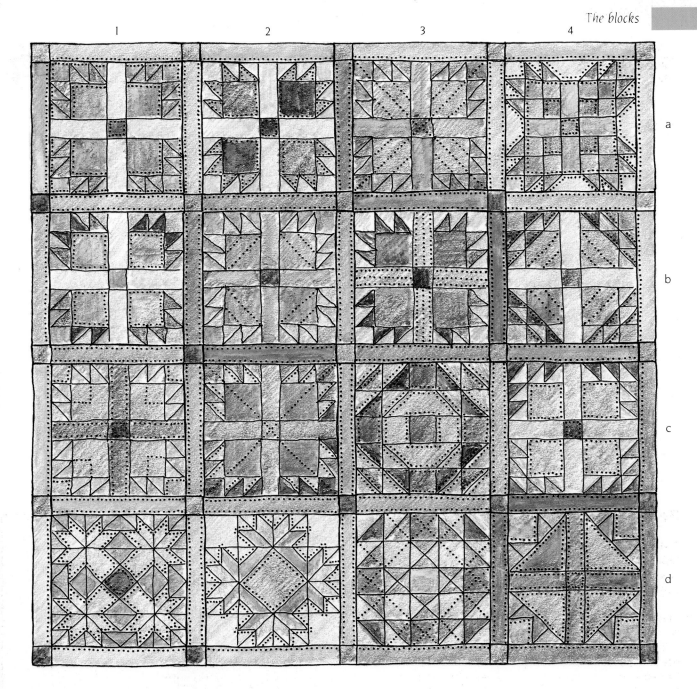

101 *Colour and simple quilting suggestions for* Bear's Paw *along with* The
Best Friend *(4a),* Dove in the Window *(4b),* George Town Circle
(3c), Hens and Chickens *(4c),* Devil's Claw *(1d),* Friendship Knot
(2d), Handy Andy *(3d) and* Mexican Star *(4d) reading from top right*

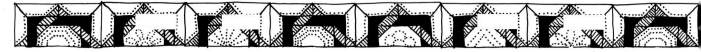

102 Interlocking Squares

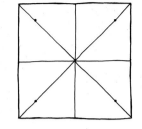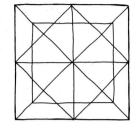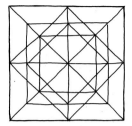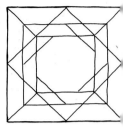

103a *The stages of drawing* Interlocking Squares

Interlocking Squares

The *Interlocking Squares* block, like the *Card Trick* block (p. 38), is illusionary. The squares intertwine with one another if you use suitable fabrics. Draw the block to size, and mark the diagonal and quarter lines. Mark a point on the diagonals half the length of the side of your block from the centre of the block. Join the ends of the quarter lines to make the first square. Join the points on the diagonal lines to make the second square. Draw in the inside of the first square by joining the points up where the second square crosses the quarter lines. Draw in the second square by joining up the points where the outside of the first square crosses the diagonals. Rub out any lines not required for the construction of the block and sort out where the tone contrasts are needed to be sure that the squares interlock. Make your templates, cut out your fabric pieces and assemble the block in the order shown.

The ordering of shapes, colours and tones to make the blocks appear three-dimensional can be very satisfying. Use fabrics that contrast in tone or colour for the squares and a fabric that does not compete with these for the background. There are many blocks that will give a three-dimensional design when dark, medium and light coloured fabrics are strategically placed. If this fascinates you, first use coloured crayons and squared paper to experiment with the blocks by colouring in the shapes in a variety of ways until you manage to make the block designs undulate.

103b *The order of piecing the block*

104 Interlocking Squares *blocks showing various ways of working*

105 *Sampler quilt by Pat Salt in a range of blue cotton fabrics with 9in square blocks*

5

The blocks completed

Once the blocks are all finished, a decision has to be made about the layout of the quilt. Find a large space where you can lay all the blocks out flat. A bed will not do because it is impossible to see all the blocks together and allow for various arrangements to be made. I move my furniture to one side and lay a quilt out on the carpet. This is all very well if you have a big enough house, but perhaps you can ask a friend for their advice and at the same time for the use of their carpet space. Most people are very pleased to see and admire the work. Another large space might be found in a classroom. Take advantage of any space when it is available.

It is a good idea to ask other people for their advice about the layout because this often determines for you what you really think. I know that if someone makes a criticism about my work with which I agree or disagree, it makes me stronger in my convictions: I have noticed this also happens with my students.

It is not easy to make a symmetrical layout of the blocks. The patterns and colour of the individual blocks with their borders are so varied that it is probably easier to balance them by eye. Some of you will have favourite blocks and you can start by placing these in a prominent position. It is easiest to start with an idea and work around this.

Having decided on the layout of the blocks in the quilt, mark their position in some way. Pin a number to each block and keep a plan of this numbered arrangement. It is only too easy to make a mistake while assembling the blocks. Once you have made your plan, begin assembling the quilt. Do not worry about the decision; a quilt is a big item and the sooner you begin the work the more satisfied you will feel with its progress.

Follow the method of assembly of the blocks into the flat quilt shown earlier in the book. At this time you are dealing with larger sections of the quilt and it becomes heavier to manage, so think how you will deal with this situation. If you work at a table which supports the quilt at all times, then you will not find that the quilt is being pulled away from you by its own weight. It is easy to bend your back or hold your arms up in an awkward position for long periods of time without realizing it. So take precautions.

At this stage you will know if your calculations on the size of the quilt are correct or whether you now have to add an extra border to bring it up to size. When you quilt something it tends to contract in size, depending on how much quilting you do; it is difficult to allow for this in your calculation. Look at the section on borders to give you some ideas of what sort of border you would like to add.

6

Bordering and finishing the quilt

A quilt made of individual blocks that have their own borders does not necessarily need an overall border. A simple straight binding, or the edges of the quilt top and backing turned in on themselves, may be all that is needed.

It is possible to unite the whole quilt by using in the border a piece of every fabric used in the quilt. The colour from the fabrics supports that in the blocks. Unity can also be gained by using one of the many shape ideas from the blocks of the quilt. Illustrated here and with the sections on blocks are some border designs taken from ideas within the blocks. Think carefully about the corner of a border so that difficulties are not made for the 'quilt-as-you-go' technique.

A series of narrow and wide strips of fabric as a border can act like a picture frame for the quilt. Decide which colour is the most important in the quilt and choose coloured fabrics for the borders that are supporting and so give more emphasis to the main colour. There are numerous variations on this theme, and it is easy to make up the quilt to just the correct size using strips of fabric in this way.

It can be quite difficult to find the right way to turn the border round the corners of the quilt. This can be resolved by having two short borders and two longer ones and not getting into difficulties with trying to make mitred corners. The short ones are added first, followed by the longer ones. The other way to resolve the problem of the corners is to make the border fit each side of the quilt and then fill the corner in with a square. This could be all of one fabric, or a block pattern such as one used in the quilt. Another idea is to take a quarter of a block and place one quarter in each corner. The *Four Baskets* would easily divide into quarters to make this arrangement.

A square quilt can be made into a rectangular one by adding an extra border to opposite ends before adding the final border.

A simple quilted border gives a gentle edge to the quilt if the quilting from the blocks or the block borders is repeated in the main border.

Naming the quilt

While bordering the quilt, think about labelling it. It may be interesting to future generations to know who made the quilt, and for whom, when, where and why the quilt was made. The labelling need not be intrusive on the design of the quilt, or it can be made part of the design features of one of the blocks. It could be included with the quilting, hand embroidered in cross-stitch or some other appropriate stitch, machine embroidered, or written with a pen. I have seen all these methods of labelling used satisfactorily. I make a fabric label, machine stitch the wording on it and then hand sew this to the back of the quilt.

It is a good idea to give your quilt a name if you intend to exhibit it. The more quilts you make, the easier it is to refer to a quilt by name rather than the 'pink one' or the 'blue one', or 'sampler quilt 1' or 'sampler quilt 2'.

106 Eight border ideas based on the designs within blocks that might be
included in the quilt

7

More quilts to make

Once you have finished the sampler quilt you will have twenty-five sets of templates, which could be the beginning of a lifetime of making quilts. Throughout the section on blocks in this book there are beginnings of ideas for how an individual block can be the start of an entire quilt. The illustrations show how blocks can be placed directly next to one another or with a lattice between the blocks. The 'quilt-as-you-go' method is one that can be used even if you do not have borders around each individual block. The quilting around the edge of each block or section must be left undone until these are joined. The sections do not have to be the same shape or size, but you need to be able to assemble them without sewing around a corner. This requires a little time spent working out the order of assembly of the sections of the quilt at the planning stage.

107 A small sampler quilt by Elizabeth Rowe made in fine cotton lawn fabric
with flanelette sheet used as an interlining

Further reading

Quiltmaking in Patchwork and Appliqué
  Michele Walker
  Ebury Press 1985
  ISBN 0 85223 433 3

The Perfect Patchwork Primer
  Beth Gutcheon
  David McKay Co. Inc. 1973
  Penguin Books 1974

The Standard Book of Quiltmaking and Collecting
  Marguerite Ikis
  Dover Publications Inc. 1949

The Quilter's Album of Blocks and Borders
  Jinny Beyer
  EPM Publications Inc. 1980
  Bell & Hyman, London
  ISBN 0 7135 1345 4

Patchwork Patterns
  Jinny Beyer
  EPM Publications Inc. 1979
  Bell & Hyman, London 1984
  ISBN 0 7135 1346 2

The Complete Book of Patchwork and Quilting
  WI Books Ltd., London
  ISBN 0 947990 00 3

The Quiltmaker's Handbook
  Michael James
  A Spectrum Book, Prentice-Hall Inc.
  ISBN 0 13 749408 4

Patchwork
  Averil Colby
  B. T. Batsford Ltd., London
  ISBN 0 7134 5770 8

Patchwork, Quilting and Appliqué
  Linda Seward
  Mitchell Beazley Publisher
  ISBN 0 8553 3663 3

Useful addresses

Crafts of Quality Books
1 Wingrad House, Jubilee Street, London E1 3BJ

Craft Publications
Westbury Mill, Westbury, Nr. Brackley, Northants, NN13 5JS

Pioneer Patches
Marsh Lane, Huddersfield, HD3 4AB

Strawberry Fayre
Chagford, Devon, TQ13 8EN

The Quilt Room
20 West Street, Dorking, Surrey, RH4 1BL

Village Fabrics
30 Goldsmith's Lane, Wallingford, Oxon., OX10 0DN

The Quilters' Guild,
The Secretary, 25 Churchfields, Tickton, Beverley, North Humberside, HU17 9SX, England

American Quilter's Society
P.O. Box 3290, Paducah, Kentucky 42001, USA

Gutcheon Patchworks Inc.
584 Broadway, New York, NY 10012, USA

Quilts and Other Comforts
Box 394-4, 6700 West 44th Avenue, Wheatridge, CO 80034-0394, USA

My local shop is ever willing to serve its customers as are many local shops. These often have a greater variety of stock than bigger shops.

English/American glossary

card . . . cardboard
calico . . . muslin
centre . . . center
colour . . . color
domett . . . a woven cloth originally with a cotton warp and a woollen weft
flannelette sheet . . . an outing flannel sheet or cotton flannel sheet

furnishing cotton . . . cotton curtain fabric
interlining or wadding . . . stuffing, filler, batting or padding
layout paper or greaseproof paper . . . thin paper or tracing paper
a pair of compasses . . . compass
poly-cotton . . . mixed fibre fabric
rag bag . . . scrap bag
tack . . . baste

Index